discover countries

Afghanistan

Richard Spilsbury

WAYLAND

First published in 2011 by Wayland
Copyright Wayland 2011

Wayland
Hachette Children's Books
338 Euston Road
London NW1 3BH

Wayland Australia
Level 17/207 Kent Street,
Sydney, NSW 2000

Concept design: Jason Billin
Editors: Nicola Edwards and Jennifer Sanderson
Designer: Amy Sparks
Picture Research: Amy Sparks
Consultant: Elaine Jackson

Produced for Wayland by
White-Thomson Publishing Ltd

www.wtpub.co.uk
+44 (0)843 2087 460

British Library Cataloguing in Publication Data
Spilsbury, Richard, 1963-
Afghanistan -- (Discover countries)
1. Afghanistan -- Juvenile literature.
I. Title II. Series   958.1'047-dc22

ISBN: 978 07502 6448 8
Printed in Malaysia

Wayland is a division of Hachette Children's Books
an Hachette UK company
www.hachette.co.uk

All data in this book was researched in 2010
and has been collected from the latest sources available at that time.

Contents

Discovering Afghanistan

Afghanistan is a mountainous country in central Asia that is about two-and-a-half times as big as the UK. It is a poor country, damaged by years of fighting, and is struggling to improve its economy.

A new regime

After years of political turmoil following invasion by the Soviet Union in 1979, the Taliban party took control of Afghanistan in 1996. The Taliban was popular among many people because it promised peace. However, it brought in some harsh rules. The Taliban punished people by public flogging and execution.

Afghanistan Statistics

Area: 652,230 sq km (251,827 sq miles)

Capital city: Kabul

Government type: Islamic Republic

Bordering countries: China, Iran, Pakistan, Tajikistan, Turkmenistan, Uzbekistan

Currency: Afghani (AFA)

Language: Afghan Persian or Dari (official) 50%, Pashto (official) 35%, Turkic languages (primarily Uzbek and Turkmen) 11%, 30 minor languages (primarily Balochi and Pashai) 4%

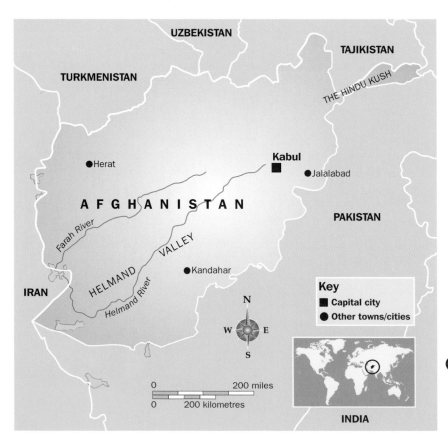

🔵 Afghanistan is a land-locked country, that borders Pakistan to the east and Iran to the west. The countries to the north of Afghanistan were once part of the Soviet Union.

Girls were not allowed to go to school and women could not work. It also welcomed terrorist groups, such as Osama Bin Laden's Al Qaeda, into the country.

Election

After the Al Qaeda attacks in 2001 on the Twin Towers in New York, USA, US and UK forces invaded Afghanistan. They toppled the Taliban and helped anti-Taliban forces take power. In 2004, Hamid Karzai became Afghanistan's first democratically elected president. In recent years, life has improved for many people in Afghanistan. For example, all children have a better chance of a good education. However, since 2008, troops from the United Nations (UN) have been fighting against Taliban forces that have re-emerged in Afghanistan.

Future challenges

Afghanistan's weak economy is partly a result of its troubled recent history. The country has also been unable to invest in and profit from its oil, gas, and other natural resources. This means that its people rely on foreign help, such as food aid. In the future, Afghans hope that a stable government will bring peace and security to their country. This will help the economy recover and the country's dramatic scenery and tribal peoples might attract visitors and more investment.

Although Kabul bears the scars of the country's past turmoil, reconstruction is making it a busy capital city.

DID YOU KNOW?

Hundreds of tanks lie rusting near Kabul. They were abandoned when the Soviet Union, which had since 1979, left in 1989.

Landscape and climate

Afghanistan is a land-locked country with no coastline. In spring, its many rivers are filled by melted snow from the mountains. However, there is limited fresh water available in summer because there are few lakes and most rivers dry up.

High and low

A spine of high mountains stretches from the north-east to the south-west of Afghanistan. These mountains include the Hindu Kush, which borders Northern Pakistan and Tajikistan, the high Pamirs, bordering China, and smaller mountains that run more centrally (see map on page 4). There are flatter regions near the borders of Iran in the south-west and Turkmenistan and Uzbekistan in the north. The mountains are a factor making the Afghanistan government weak. This is because Afghans living in mountainous areas are isolated from Kabul and often ruled by local tribal leaders.

Facts at a glance

Land area: 652,230 sq km (251,827 sq miles)

Highest point: Noshak 7,485 m (24,557 ft)

Lowest point: Amu Darya 258m (846 ft)

Longest river: Helmand River 1150km long (715 miles)

🔻 Although the thick snow on mountains in Afghanistan is beautiful, it blocks roads and causes avalanches threatening settlements.

► In spring and summer, snowmelt fills the rivers in Afghanistan's mountain valleys.

Climate

Afghanistan has a continental climate. This means that it has warm, dry summers and very cold, snowy winters. The country gets most of its rain in spring. The mountains prevent the summer monsoon winds that blow from the Indian Ocean from reaching Afghanistan. In summer, the flatter regions of the south-west become very hot, dry and dusty.

Extreme weather

The country also suffers some extreme weather events. In summer in the south and the west, the hot, dry 'wind of 120 days' brings intense heat and drought and can cause sand storms. It carries dust and can reach speeds of up to 180 km/h (110 m/h). This wind makes farming difficult and causes life-threatening health conditions in people, such as heat stroke. In the mountains there are frequent blizzards in winter.

DID YOU KNOW? The first windmills were invented in Afghanistan, Iran and Iraq. These used the winds that blow from the mountains over the plains to grind grain.

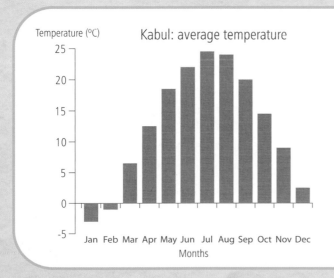

Temperature (°C) — Kabul: average temperature — Months

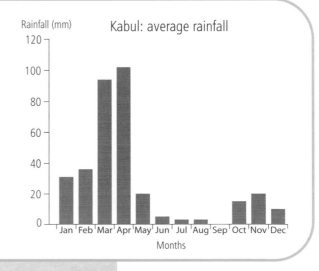

Rainfall (mm) — Kabul: average rainfall — Months

Population and health

Afghanistan has a growing population that is made up of a variety of tribal peoples. Almost all Afghans face health challenges.

Changing population

The majority of people in Afghanistan are quite young because families tend to have many children. According to the UN, the population was 28 million in 2009 and could grow to more than 110 million by 2050. The population has gone up and down in the past because of violence and war. In the 1980s and 90s, hundreds of thousands of people left to escape the fighting, but many have since returned.

⬤ Young people make up the majority of many Afghan communities. Nearly half the population is 14 years old or younger.

Tribal groups

There are many tribal groups in Afghanistan. The Pashtuns are the largest group and are found in the south and the east. Traditionally, Pashtuns are farmers and they speak Pashto. The Tajik people in the north-east are traditionally traders. They speak Dari. The main groups in north-central Afghanistan are the Hazaras, Tajiks and Uzbeks. Across the country, more than 30 different languages are spoken and many people are bilingual.

Facts at a glance

Total population: 28.2 million

Life expectancy at birth: 45 years

Children dying before the age of five: 25.7%

Ethnic composition: Pashtun 42%, Tajik 27%, Hazara 9%, Uzbek 9%, Aimak 4%, Turkmen 3%, Baloch 2%, other 4%

Health, dangers and disease

There are few doctors and hospitals in Afghanistan. One-sixth of Afghans have no access to any healthcare. The country has one of the world's highest infant, child and maternal mortality rates. Seventy per cent of Afghans have no access to clean water and so the risk of catching infectious diseases, such as diarrhoea and typhoid, from dirty water is high. Another danger is from land mines left by Soviet and other foreign troops in the past. There are 30 times more amputations each year in Afghanistan than there are in the USA because people accidentally step on or pick up the abandoned land mines.

Afghanistan: age structure of the population

- 65 years and over: 2%
- 0–14 years: 43%
- 15-64 years: 55%

Afghanistan: population growth, 1960-2050

Population (millions)

Years

Projected

In a busy Afghan clinic, a young amputee waits to be fitted with a replacement leg so that he can walk again.

DID YOU KNOW?
Many Afghans now speak some English and new words have been invented. For example, 'gadwad' is Pashto for messy and the new word 'gadwadation' means a messy situation.

Settlements and living

During the years of war since the 1980s, about half a million homes were destroyed, as well as power plants, hospitals and other buildings. With foreign help, the Afghans are rebuilding their settlements.

Rural and urban

More people are moving to Afghanistan's cities every year. This is partly because foreign organizations have paid to rebuild streets ruined by war and this has created many jobs. Some farmers have moved to the cities because of failing crops, for example after a long spell of drought in 2000. People are also leaving some rural areas because of fighting with the Taliban.

Facts at a glance

Urban population: 22.4% (6.3 million)

Rural population: 77.6% (21.9 million)

Population of largest city: 3.3 million (Kabul)

Houses in this traditional mountain village are clustered together for shelter. Despite the dry landscape, the trees are a sign that a river flows through the valley.

Poor housing

Around one-third of Afghans live in inadequate or low-grade housing. This is partly because there is a shortage of building materials. It is also because, when more people move to the cities, the demand for land increases and landowners put up prices. There are slums surrounding Kabul where the population has increased six times since 2001. Many new homes are badly built and have poor water and electricity supply. Some, such as those on hills surrounding Kabul, are at risk from floods and avalanches.

Settlements

In the countryside, most of the villages are built on the plains or in valleys. The villages are usually near rivers so that people have a supply of fresh water. In villages, many families live in small, rectangular, mud-brick houses.
The biggest cities are Kabul, Kandahar to the south-west, and Mazar-e-Sharif and Herat to the north and west. Afghanistan's cities are home to around twenty per cent of the population, with 11 per cent in Kabul alone. In cities, many people live in cramped apartment blocks.

DID YOU KNOW? Organizations such as the Federation for American Scientists are developing polystyrene houses for Afghans. These are light, easy to construct, and can survive the shaking caused by the earthquakes that happen there each year.

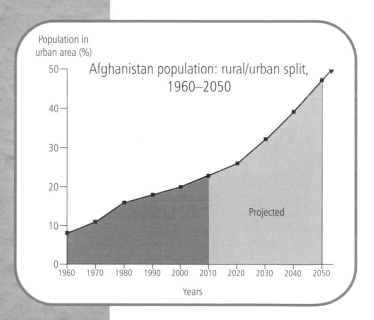

Population in urban area (%)

Afghanistan population: rural/urban split, 1960–2050

Projected

Years

Family life

There may be many different tribes and languages spoken in Afghanistan, but family life is much the same across the country. Families are close-knit and spend most of their time together.

The Afghan family

Many Afghans live in extended family groups. The head of the family is the oldest man, or patriarch. With him live his wife, their unmarried daughters, their sons, and their sons' wives and children. Younger members of the family are expected to show respect to older members and to always do as they are told. The family lives together in one home or in buildings in a shared compound. In city households, many families also have cousins or other relatives from the countryside staying with them. Under Taliban rule, only men went out to work and women looked after the family and the home, but this is changing as more women are employed.

▶ Afghan men typically live in the same homes as their children and grandchildren and have a great influence over their lives.

Facts at a glance

Average children per childbearing woman:
5.5 children

Average household size:
8 people

12

● These women and children are at a wedding in Arghandab, Kandahar. They are wearing traditional embroidered clothing and special jewellery.

Getting married

Patriarchs often choose partners for their children. This may be arranged a long time before the wedding, when they are still children. Sometimes, the bride and groom do not meet until the wedding day. Weddings last for days and include music, feasts and different ceremonies. For example, the day before a wedding, the groom gives henna to his bride. She then has a 'henna party', where her female relatives make intricate henna patterns on her hands.

Children

Once they are married, most wives move in with their husband's family. Couples usually have several children. The older children are expected to look after younger children in the family. In the past, many Afghan men had up to four wives, but this is less common now. Divorce is rare. When a father dies, his sons usually share any inheritance. Daughters and widows seldom inherit any money or property. They have to depend on their brothers' or sons' generosity.

DID YOU KNOW?
Families have special feasts when boys reach the age of seven. At this age, boys are usually circumcised and they are allowed to wear a turban, like the adult men, for the first time.

Religion and beliefs

Afghanistan's full name is 'The Islamic Republic of Afghanistan'. Religion and belief in Islam shape almost every aspect of the Afghan people's lives.

Islam in Afghanistan

Around 1,500 years ago, many people in Afghanistan followed the Buddhist religion. This changed when the Islamic Empire spread into the region in the seventh century. Today, 99 per cent of people in Afghanistan are Muslim. Most are Sunni Muslims but the Hazara people are Shiite Muslims. Sunni and Shiite Muslims follow different leaders and worship at different shrines or mosques. Sunni Taliban leaders persecuted Shiites when they were in power. Today, the government tries to prevent clashes by making sure there are some Shiite Muslims in government.

DID YOU KNOW?
In 2001, members of the Taliban blew up two 55-metre-high statues of Buddha in the mountainside at Bamiyan. The Taliban destroyed these ancient, world-famous statues because they were not Islamic.

🔻 Female followers of Islam in Afghanistan often wear body-covering garments, such as a burka, when outside their home – for example while visiting markets.

The mullah

Mullahs are male Islamic religious leaders. They deliver Friday sermons and prayers in mosques, carry out marriages and funerals, and teach Islamic laws and beliefs. They are trusted community leaders in Afghanistan who help to sort out disputes and give advice on health matters, such as contraception. In 2009, the Afghanistan government trained mullahs to make more Afghan men aware of women's rights.

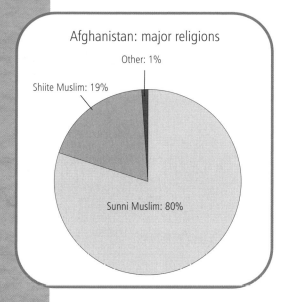

Afghanistan: major religions

Other: 1%
Shiite Muslim: 19%
Sunni Muslim: 80%

Festivals

Two of the most important Islamic festivals in Afghanistan are Eid-el-Fitr and Eid-ul-Adha. Eid-el-Fitr marks the end of Ramadan. During Ramadan, Muslims do not eat or drink between sunrise and sunset. They do this to honour the time when the Qu'ran was revealed to the prophet Muhammad. During Eid-el-Fitr there are services in mosques and families eat a special meal. Eid-ul-Adha remembers that the prophet Abraham was willing to sacrifice his son when God ordered him to. Muslims sacrifice a goat as a symbol of what Abraham was prepared to do.

The Islamic New Year is in March and is known as Nowruz. Afghans usually celebrate with family picnics and by eating desserts, such as *haft-mehwah*. This contains fruit and nuts that symbolize the arrival of spring.

Afghan men in Kabul have a meal of beans and rice to break their religious fast at dusk during Ramadan.

Education and learning

The years of Soviet occupation, Taliban rule and war with Allied forces, severely damaged education in Afghanistan. Schools were bombed and many teachers fled the country. Today, schools are being rebuilt and more children have the chance to learn.

Schools in Afghanistan

In 1996, there were only 650 public schools in the country. Religious schools, called madrassas, were the main centres of learning. After 2001, foreign aid was used to rebuild the education system. By 2008, six million children were enrolled at more than 9,000 schools. However, many children still miss out. Some schools do not have enough trained teachers. Some children live in the mountains, too far from a school. The Taliban also continues to threaten teachers and bomb schools, especially girls' schools.

Facts at a glance

Children in primary school:
Male 74%, Female 46%

Children in secondary school:
not known

Literacy rate (over 15 years):
28%

▼ These girls are taking part in the opening ceremony of a new girls' school in 2009. In good weather, some lessons take place outside, but the new building means school can continue when it is raining or snowing.

Adult education

Recently, there has been an increase in adult education programmes. For example, theatre groups travel to remote villages to teach people things such as healthcare and how to get financial help from the government. Many of these courses are aimed at women. This is important because if women are educated, they can teach their daughters. Out of the eight universities in Afghanistan, the biggest is Kabul University, with around 20,000 students. In 2009 a quarter of students at Afghan universities were women.

Literacy

Fewer than one-third of Afghans can read and write. One reason for this is that there are not many schools. The other problem is that most girls spend only four years at school. Some girls are expected to help cook, clean and look after younger brothers and sisters. Some Muslims do not send their daughters to school because they do not think that girls, especially older girls, should mix with boys. Due to this lack of education, only 12 per cent of the women in Afghanistan can read and write.

▶ Children in Afghanistan still study the Qu'ran in mosques or madrassas. Boys and girls usually study separately.

Employment and economy

In Afghanistan, 70 per cent of the people live on less than US$2 a day. However, the economy is slowly improving as money from foreign governments and charities is helping to pay for rebuilding. This is creating more jobs, although one-third of the Afghan people are still unemployed.

Jobs

One of the main causes for the high unemployment in Afghanistan is the damage done to industries by the years of war and Taliban rule. Another is that many adults are uneducated and cannot apply for some types of job.

Some industries in Afghanistan are improving, though. For example, there are more shops, hotels and restaurants today. These cater for Afghans and foreign visitors working in construction, security, or for charities. Gradually more and more women are working, too. Now there are female teachers, lawyers and politicians. This is a stark contrast to the Taliban years when women were banned from working. However, women still make up less than 30 per cent of the workforce.

▲ Bakeries like this one in Kabul are part of Afghanistan's growing service industry.

Facts at a glance

Contributions to GDP:
agriculture: 31%
industry: 26%
services: 43%

Labour force:
agriculture: 78.6%
industry: 5.7%
services: 15.7%

Female labour force:
27% of total

Unemployment rate: 35%

Black market

The buying and selling of illegal goods is known as the black market. Black market trade makes up over half of Afghanistan's gross domestic product (GDP). The biggest earner is the production and sale of opium, a drug made from poppy flowers.

The opium trade is worth over US$4 billion each year. Most of the heroin that is used by drug-takers in Europe and Eurasia comes from Afghan opium, and nearly a quarter of a million Afghans also use the drug. Many countries want Afghanistan to stop producing opium to help solve the world's drug problem. UN soldiers have been destroying Afghan poppy fields. However, for many farmers growing poppies is still the easiest way to make money.

These British soldiers, who are part of UN forces in Afghanistan, are patrolling a poppy field in Helmand province. This area is an important opium producing area fiercely defended by Taliban fighters.

Industry and trade

In the past, Afghanistan was occupied or ruled by many other countries, including Greece, the Soviet Union and Britain. The countries wanted control of this region because of its position on trading routes between the East and West. Today, lorries carry goods on routes through Afghanistan to neighbouring countries.

Natural resources

Afghanistan has several valuable natural resources – for example, fossil fuels including oil and gas, metals such as copper, iron and gold, and emeralds and other gemstones. In the past, mining and changing these resources into goods for export were important industries. Afghanistan used to export oil to the Soviet Union and made fertilizers from gas and coal.

Although coal is mined, Afghanistan has other natural resources that are not exploited due to a lack of investment in mines.

However, during the long periods of war, the oil and gas wells were blocked up to prevent damage and these industries virtually died out. There are plans to reopen these wells after the fighting has stopped. Today, foreign businesses are investing in some mines. For example, Chinese companies are paying to open up copper and iron mines.

Industries

Most industries in Afghanistan use resources grown on its farms to produce goods. Some goods, such as leather shoes and soap, are sold within the country. Exported goods include sugar, salt, cotton textiles and carpets. Carpet making is the country's most valuable legal export. In 2007, approximately one million Afghans worked in the carpet industry. Many more had jobs keeping sheep to provide wool for the carpet makers.

Industries and factories sometimes face problems with power supply. Most of Afghanistan's electricity is supplied by neighbouring countries such as Tajikistan. The supply is limited and there are often blackouts when no electricity gets through to homes and businesses.

▼ Carpet weaving is often carried on a small scale by Afghan women. Carpets are also made in large factories.

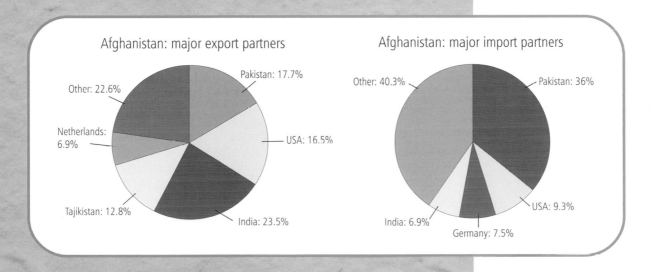

Afghanistan: major export partners

Other: 22.6%
Pakistan: 17.7%
Netherlands: 6.9%
USA: 16.5%
Tajikistan: 12.8%
India: 23.5%

Afghanistan: major import partners

Other: 40.3%
Pakistan: 36%
India: 6.9%
Germany: 7.5%
USA: 9.3%

Farming and food

About one-tenth of Afghan land is farmed. Much farmland was damaged during the wars. Some land has land mines in it and some was polluted when oil pipes were damaged. Farmland has also been damaged by overgrazing. In some areas there is not enough rainfall or irrigation to grow food.

Crops and livestock

Most farmers are subsistence farmers. They grow just enough food for their families and sell any that is left over. Afghan farmers grow wheat, barley and rice.

Afghan farmers plant rice shoots in flooded fields. The country produces around 70 per cent of the rice it needs, importing the rest from Pakistan and Iran.

They farm fruits such as apricots, dates and grapes, nuts including pistachios, and spices such as saffron. The main growing areas are in the south where the land is more fertile. Livestock farmers raise cattle, goats and fat-tailed sheep.

Helping farmers

Many poor farmers grow poppies rather than food crops (see page 19). Taliban and tribal leaders often give farmers money in advance for this valuable crop. Today, the government encourages these farmers to grow food crops instead by offering to lend them money to buy seeds and tools. The government also helps farmers to find buyers for their produce, for example selling pomegranates to Iran.

Food

The staple food of Afghanistan is wheat, which people use to make flatbread and dumplings. Rice is also very popular, and is used to make the national dish of spiced rice called pullao. Most of the wheat is imported. This means that Afghans are badly affected when wheat prices rise. Most Afghans do not eat much meat but instead include plenty of vegetables, such as potatoes and spinach, and lots of yoghurt in their diet. Across the country, one-third of Afghans do not eat enough healthy food to lead full and active lives. In some areas, charities give free school meals to children and food to take home.

DID YOU KNOW?

In the past, Afghans celebrated the annual pistachio harvest with festivals and huge community picnics in the wild pistachio forests.

In drier regions of Afghanistan, where grazing land is sparse, rearing sheep is one of the most widespread types of farming.

Transport and communications

In the countryside, most people travel and carry goods on foot or on carts pulled by horses and donkeys. In cities, people use taxis, buses, lorries and rickshaws. There are only about half a million private cars in Afghanistan.

Roads

Afghanistan's road system is one of the worst in the world. Some of the roads that were destroyed during the Soviet occupation and wars have been rebuilt. However, roads can be dangerous because few drivers have passed tests and vehicles are often in poor condition or overloaded. The steep road from Kabul to Jalalabad that runs along the edge of deep gorges is thought to be the most dangerous in the world.

▼ Afghanistan's rough, narrow mountain roads have few safety barriers, so drivers are at risk from accidents and from falling rocks.

DID YOU KNOW?
When snow blocks the only road over the Hindu Kush, lorries bring supplies to communities there through the Salang Tunnel, the world's second highest road tunnel.

Rail, air and sea

Afghan rulers in the past refused to build railways for fear that they would be used by foreign invaders. However, in 2010 the first ever railway line in Afghanistan was completed between Mazar-e-Sharif and Uzbekistan. Although airports were destroyed by wars, there are now 42 airports of different sizes and a national airline, called Ariana. Afghanistan is 2,000 kilometres from the sea but Afghan ships transport goods in and out of the Arabian Sea port of Chabahar, Iran.

Communication

The first mobile telephones in Afghanistan went on sale in 2001. By 2006, there were more than 3 million users. Today around 600,000 people use the Internet, mostly in Internet cafes or in schools. Using the Internet has made many people more aware of life in other countries and cultures. This is making some people question traditional Afghan customs, such as whether men and women should be allowed to meet openly in public.

▶ In Afghanistan in 2001, the price of placing a call from a mobile telephone was $2 a minute. However, it now costs 10 cents a minute to call and even less to send a text message.

▼ These Afghan men are being trained to use computers in a Jalalabad school. Computer education for children and adults can provide both job skills and access to global information.

Afghanistan: Internet and mobile phone use, 1995–2008

Millions

Mobile phones in use

Internet subscribers

Years: 1995, 2000, 2005, 2008

Leisure and tourism

During the Taliban years, many leisure activities were stopped – for example, it was against the law for people to fly kites, and women were banned from sports centres. Today, such bans have been lifted and women take part in many activities and sports, including martial arts.

Leisure

Afghanistan's national sport is buzkashi, which is played mostly in northern Afghanistan. In buzkashi, teams of men on horseback try to lift a headless calf and put it into a scoring area. Afghans also enjoy football and a type of wrestling called ghosai.

▼ Buzkashi matches are rough and can last for days. They usually happen at special events including carnivals, when wrestling bouts also take place.

Cricket is also becoming popular after it was brought into the country by refugees returning from Pakistan. Today, kite-makers are back in business and the skies are once more filled with colourful kite battles. Kite flying is a game in which people try to cut opponents' kite strings using their own, which are often coated with ground glass and flour glue. Many Afghans also enjoy live music, going to the theatre and to poetry readings, as well as watching television and going to the cinema.

Tourism

For most Afghans, a holiday means visiting relatives within the country. Few people can afford to travel abroad. At present, not many tourists from abroad visit Afghanistan either. This is because of the threat posed by war between UN forces and the Taliban, and because there is not yet a tourist industry. However, there are tourist attractions, such as the blue mosques in the ancient city of Mazar-e-Sharif and the dramatic mountain scenery.

In future, the country hopes to attract tourists to bring in money and development. In the 1960s and 1970s Afghanistan had been a climbing centre, and today, some mountaineering companies are starting trips in the high northern mountain areas where there are unclimbed peaks and good weather for climbing.

▶ Climbing expeditions such as this one in the Pamirs bring in tourist income for Afghan locals, including guides and hotel owners.

Environment and wildlife

Afghanistan is a wild and beautiful country. Within its forests and mountains there is a wide variety of wildlife. However, Afghanistan faces a major challenge in protecting its land and its animals from the threats posed by human activities.

Deforestation

Afghanistan faces several environmental issues. One is deforestation. Today, only 1 per cent of the forests that originally covered the land remain. Although President Karzai banned tree-felling in 2006, illegal logging is still a problem, especially in eastern Afghanistan. People cut trees to use the wood for building, heating and cooking. Forests have also been affected by the long periods of drought.

The Band-e-Amir National Park was created in 2009 to help protect the wildlife of the region around the Band-e-Amir lakes.

Soil degradation

Another environmental problem is soil degradation. The hot, dry climate causes soil erosion, which is when the fertile layer of topsoil is worn away. This has been made worse by overgrazing and deforestation. In some areas, the loss of topsoil has been so bad that the land has turned to desert. This has affected livestock and damaged wildlife populations.

Wildlife

Long-horned Marco Polo sheep, golden eagles and mountain salamanders can be found in Afghanistan's mountains. In the deserts there are goitered gazelles, porcupines, and camel spiders. The country is also home to nine different types of wild cat, from snow leopards and lynx to jungle cats. This varied wildlife is threatened by habitat destruction and also hunting.

There are about 70 species in Afghanistan that are protected by law, and in 2009, the country created its first national park. Band-e-Amir is an area of deep blue lakes in the Hindu Kush Mountains that is home to important wildlife species, such as the Afghan snow finch. The governments of Afghanistan, China, Pakistan and Tajikistan are planning an international peace park to protect part of the Pamir Mountains, which link the four countries.

DID YOU KNOW?
Afghanistan is home to one of the world's least-known birds. The large-billed reed warbler was discovered in 1867 but not seen again until 2006. Today, the warblers are breeding.

▲ The borders between Afghanistan, Pakistan, and China meet in the Pamirs. Snow leopards range across these mountains, so shared protection from hunters should mean their numbers will increase.

Glossary

amputation removing limbs

circumcise cut off foreskin from penis

climate normal pattern of weather in a place

custom accepted and long-standing way of doing things

deforestation clearing land of natural woodland

democratic where decisions are made by leaders elected by others

drought long period with no or little rain, often causing a water shortage

ethnic part of a nation, race or people with shared cultural traditions. For example, Inuits are a different ethnic group to African Americans.

export transport and sell goods to another country

fertile good for growing crops

fertilizer chemical substance put on soil to make plants grow better

food aid food sent to help people in countries that are poor, especially when affected by natural disasters such as floods or conflict

fossil fuel type of fuel, such as coal or oil, that formed underground over long periods

GDP gross domestic product, which means the total value of services and goods produced by a country in a year

habitat place with particular conditions where certain types of animal and plant live

heat stroke illness caused by long periods of excessive heat

import product or service brought from one country into another

invade enter a place with military forces in order to take it over

irrigation supply water to fields in order to grow crops

land mine bomb on or under the ground that explodes when people or vehicles move over it

madrassa Islamic school

monsoon season of heavy rain in southern Asia

mortality rate the ratio of deaths in an area to the population of that area

mosque building where Muslims worship

national park area of land where habitats and other features are protected by governments for their citizens to visit

natural resources raw materials, such as fossil fuels and precious metals, that naturally occur in a place

occupied controlled by people from another country

overgrazing when there is so much livestock feeding in a place that the soil is damaged

persecute treat someone unfairly or cruelly based on their beliefs, ethnic group or other characteristic

polluted when substances added to soil, water or air make it unsafe or dirty

Qu'ran Islamic holy book

refugee person forced to leave his or her country or home because, for example, of war or natural disaster

staple food forming a large or important part of someone's daily diet

terrorist person using violence to force a government to change

turban head covering made of a long, coiled strip of cloth

United Nations (UN) association of countries aiming to improve economic, political and social conditions worldwide

Topic web

**Use this topic web to explore Afghan themes
in different areas of your curriculum.**

Design and Technology

Many kites in Afghanistan are made from multi-coloured paper with bold patterns or symbols. Design a kite of your own with an Afghan theme. For example, you could incorporate the colours of the Afghan flag in your design.

Science

Dirty water is the cause of many infectious diseases in Afghanistan. Find out more about how infectious diseases are transmitted through water. Draw a diagram to show the cycle of bacteria in water passing infectious diseases to people and how bacteria return to the water.

Maths

The unit of currency in Afghanistan is the afghani, which is divided into 100 puls. In July 2010 one US dollar was the equivalent of 46 afghanis. Most people in Afghanistan live on $14 a week. Work out what this would be in afghanis.

History

Find out what you can about the Taliban's years of rule in Afghanistan. List the ways that they wanted Afghan people to behave and some of the laws they introduced.

Afghanistan

Geography

Find out more about how the geography of Afghanistan affects the lives of the people living there and how it is a factor in keeping the country poor.

ICT

Use the Internet to research some important people in recent Afghanistan history, such as Hamid Karzai, Mullah Mohammad Omar and Osama bin Laden. How are they affecting the current political situation?

Citizenship

Afghanistan is a very poor country. Draw a spider diagram to show how richer countries could help and the different types of aid Afghanistan needs. Think about things such as roads and buildings, water and electricity supplies, health, farmers, business people, families and refugees.

English

Imagine you are a girl growing up in Afghanistan today. Write a letter to the Taliban explaining why you have a right to an education and be able to continue going to school with boys.

Further information and index

Further reading

Afghanistan (World in Focus), Nikki van den Gaag (Wayland 2009)
Afghanistan (Countries in the News), Simon Adams (Watts 2009)
Afghanistan (Welcome to my Country), Deborah Fordyce (Watts 2010)

Web

https://www.cia.gov/library/publications/the-world-factbook/geos/pk.html
Key statistics about the landscape, population, economy, government and more.
http://news.bbc.co.uk/1/hi/world/south_asia/country_profiles/1162668.stm
Country profile on Afghanistan with key facts and links to other Afghanistan websites.
http://www.guardian.co.uk/world/afghanistan
Country profile plus all the latest news on Afghanistan

Index